2nd EDITION

Textbook 1

Series editor and author: Peter Clarke

William Collins' dream of knowledge for all began with the publication of his first book in 1819.

A self-educated mill worker, he not only enriched millions of lives, but also founded a flourishing publishing house. Today, staying true to this spirit, Collins books are packed with inspiration, innovation and practical expertise.

They place you at the centre of a world of possibility and give you exactly what you need to explore it.

Collins. Freedom to teach.

Published by Collins

An imprint of HarperCollins*Publishers*
The News Building, 1 London Bridge Street, London, SE1 9GF, UK

HarperCollins*Publishers*
Macken House, 39/40 Mayor Street Upper, Dublin 1, D01 C9W8, Ireland

Browse the complete Collins catalogue at
collins.co.uk

10 9 8 7 6 5 4 3 2 1

ISBN 978-0-00-861372-3

British Library Cataloguing-in-Publication Data

A catalogue record for this publication is available from the British Library.

Series editor: Peter Clarke
Author: Peter Clarke
Product manager: Holly Woolnough
Editorial assistant: Nalisha Vansia
Copy editor: Tanya Solomons
Proofreader: Catherine Dakin
Illustrator: Ann Paganuzzi
Cover designer: Amparo Barrera
Cover illustrator: Amparo Barrera
Internal designer: 2Hoots Publishing Services
Typesetter: David Jimenez
Production controller: Alhady Ali
Printed and bound in Great Britain by Martins the Printers

Busy Ant Maths 2nd edition components are compatible with the 1st edition of Busy Ant Maths.

This book is produced from independently certified FSC™ paper to ensure responsible forest management.

For more information visit: harpercollins.co.uk/green

Acknowledgements

p9c Zhe Vasylieva/Shutterstock; p26br The Talented Bee/Shutterstock; p27tr The Talented Bee/Shutterstock; p28b Fortuna82/Shutterstock; p30b Zhe Vasylieva/Shutterstock; p49c Zhe Vasylieva/Shutterstock; p50 Fresher/Shutterstock; p58cl Vasya Kobelev/Shutterstock; p58ccl Alody/Shutterstock; p58ccr Creativika Graphics/Shutterstock; p58cr Evikka/Shutterstock; p58bcr Creativika Graphics/Shutterstock; p59c BlueRingMedia/Shutterstock; p60bl Alody/Shutterstock; p61c Pichayasri/Shutterstock; p64b Zhe Vasylieva/Shutterstock.

Contents

Multiplication and division

Fractions

Year 1 Number facts

How to use this book

This book shows different pictures, models and images (representations) to explain important mathematical ideas to do with number.

At the start of each double page is a brief description of the key mathematical ideas.

The key words related to the mathematical ideas are shown in **colour**. It's important that you understand what each of these words mean.

The main part of each double page explains the mathematical ideas. It might include pictures, models or an example.

Your teacher will talk to you about the images on the pages.

6 + 4 = 10

Sometimes there might be questions to think about or an activity to do.

Pages 6–7

This refers to mathematical ideas on other pages that you need to understand before learning about the ideas on these two pages.

Pages 12–15, 20–21, 32–47

This refers to mathematical ideas on other pages that use or build upon the ideas on these two pages.

This helps you think more deeply about the mathematical ideas.

Use the pages in this book to help you answer the questions in the Activity Books.

Read, write and count numbers to 20

We use numbers all the time. They help us count objects, add and subtract, measure, tell the time, and buy things.

Numbers can be written as **numerals** or as **words**.

A numeral is a symbol that stands for a number.

A **digit** is a symbol used to write numerals. There are 10 digits:

0 1 2 3 4 5 6 7 8 9

| 6 as a numeral | 6 as a word | numeral |

6   six   14

| digit | digit |

We can show numbers on a number track.

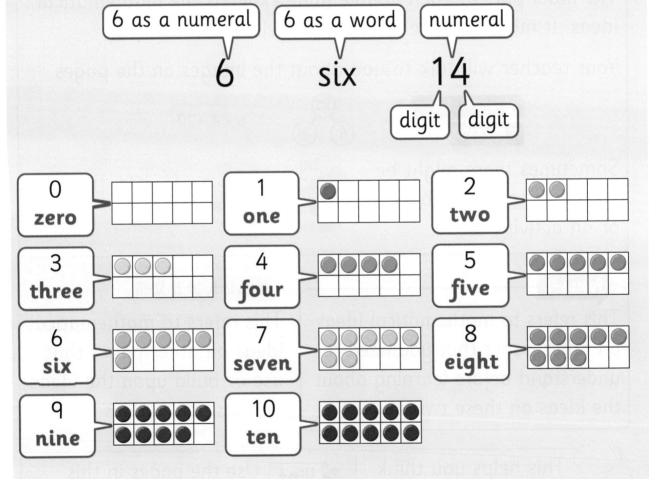

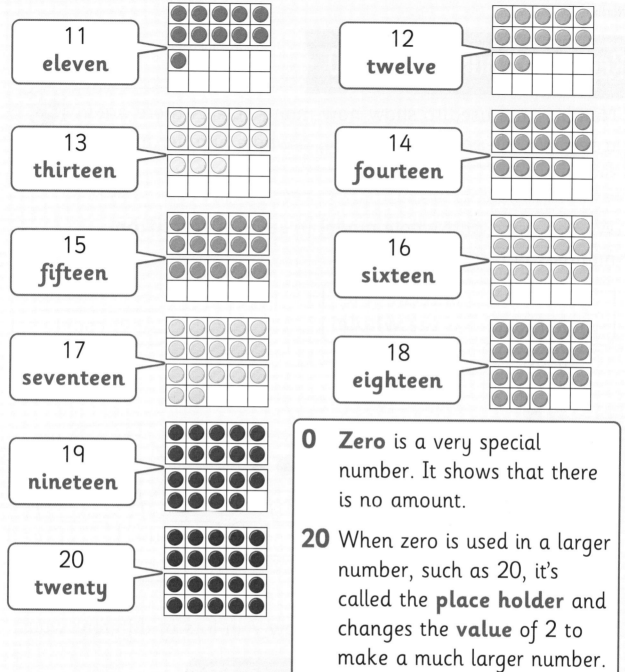

11 eleven

12 twelve

13 thirteen

14 fourteen

15 fifteen

16 sixteen

17 seventeen

18 eighteen

19 nineteen

20 twenty

0 **Zero** is a very special number. It shows that there is no amount.

20 When zero is used in a larger number, such as 20, it's called the **place holder** and changes the **value** of 2 to make a much larger number.

Say

Choose a number **less** than 10.
Count on from your number to 20.

Choose a number **greater** than 10.
Count back from your number to 0.

| 0 | 1 | 2 | 3 | 4 | 5 | 6 | 7 | 8 | 9 | 10 | 11 | 12 | 13 | 14 | 15 | 16 | 17 | 18 | 19 | 20 |

Pages 8–19, 32–61

Represent numbers to 20

Pages 6–7

Numbers are used to show how many objects there are in a set. We can split, or partition, a whole number into two or more parts.

We can use a part-whole model to split, or **partition**, numbers into two **parts**.

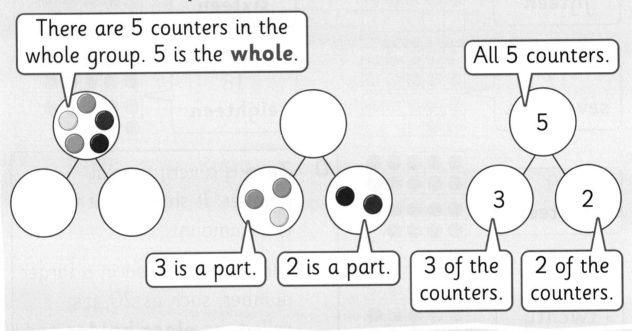

There are 5 counters in the whole group. 5 is the **whole**.

All 5 counters.

3 is a part.

2 is a part.

3 of the counters.

2 of the counters.

Look at the number 7. We can show 7 in lots of different ways.

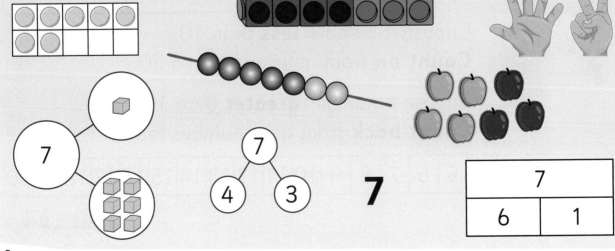

7

Look at the number 13. It has 1 ten and 3 ones.

13  1 ten — 3 ones

We can show this in lots of different ways:

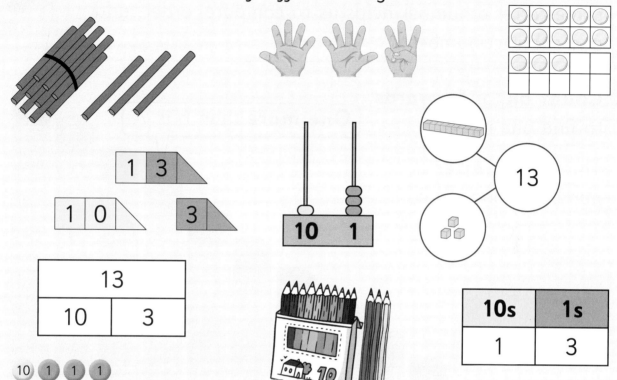

13	
10	3

10s	**1s**
1	3

11 to 20

Choose a number from 11 to 20.

How many different ways can you represent your number?

 What objects could you use?

 What pictures or models might you draw?

 Which part shows the ones?

Which part shows the tens?

How many tens and ones are there?   Pages 12–15, 20–21, 32–47

One more, one less to 20

Pages 6–7

Knowing what number comes before and what number comes after a number helps us to compare, order, add and subtract numbers.

Count on, or **forwards**, to find one more.

The number **after** a number is one more.

One more than 6 is 7.

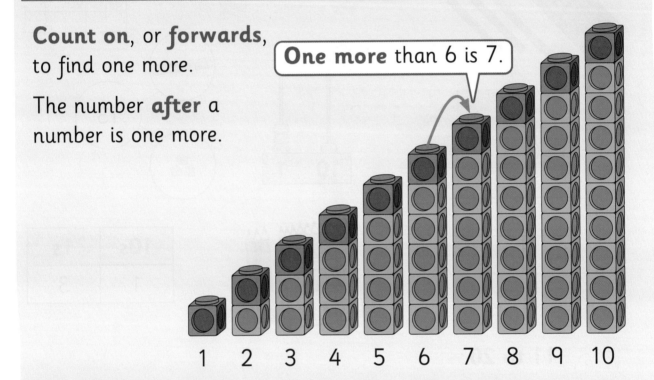

1   2   3   4   5   6   7   8   9   10

We can use a number track or number line to help find a number that is one more.

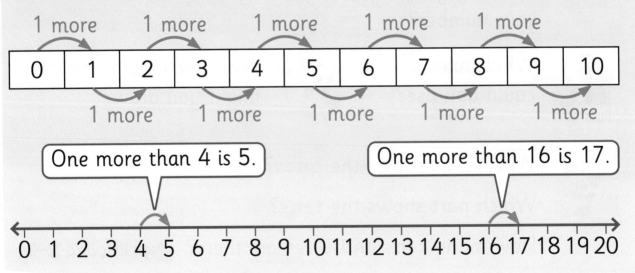

| 1 more | 1 more | 1 more | 1 more | 1 more |

| 0 | 1 | 2 | 3 | 4 | 5 | 6 | 7 | 8 | 9 | 10 |

| 1 more | 1 more | 1 more | 1 more | 1 more |

One more than 4 is 5.

One more than 16 is 17.

0 1 2 3 4 5 6 7 8 9 10 11 12 13 14 15 16 17 18 19 20

Count back, or **backwards**, to find one less.

The number **before** a number is one less.

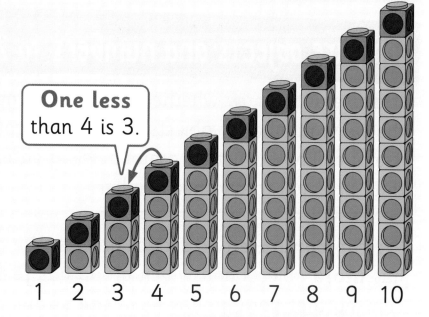

One less than 4 is 3.

We can also use a number track or number line to help find a number that is one less.

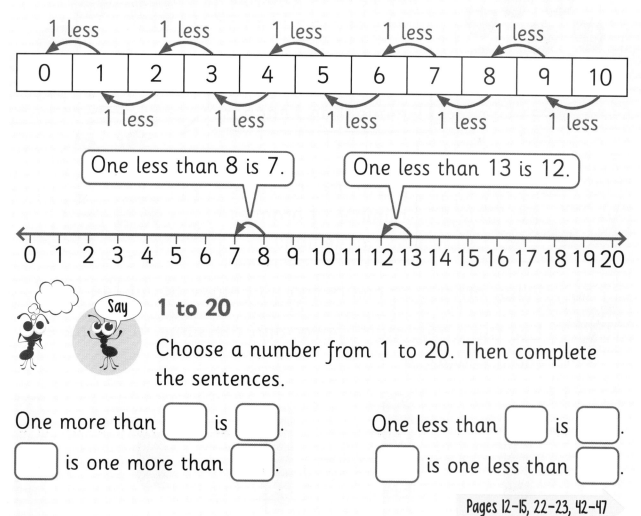

One less than 8 is 7.

One less than 13 is 12.

Say **1 to 20**

Choose a number from 1 to 20. Then complete the sentences.

One more than ☐ is ☐.

☐ is one more than ☐.

One less than ☐ is ☐.

☐ is one less than ☐.

Pages 12–15, 22–23, 42–47

Compare objects and numbers to 20

Pages 6–11

It is useful to know whether a group has more, fewer or the same number of objects as another group. It is also useful to know whether a number is greater than, less than or equal to another number.

We can **compare** two sets of objects. We can say which group has **more** objects and which group has **fewer** objects. Or we can say that both groups have **the same** number of objects.

There are more apples than oranges.

There are fewer lemons than bananas.

There are the same number of oranges as lemons.

Say What other statements can you make about the fruit?

Use the words more, fewer and the same to compare these towers of cubes.

We compare two numbers using the terms **greater than** (or **more than** or **larger than**), **less than** or **equal to**.

Look at the number of dots on each pair of dice.

5 is greater than 2.   4 is less than 6.   3 is equal to 3.

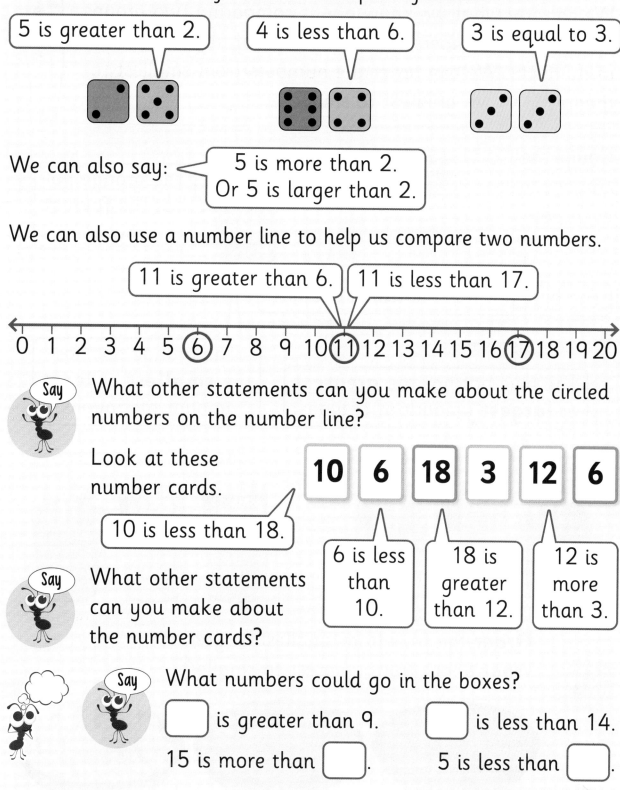

We can also say: 5 is more than 2.
Or 5 is larger than 2.

We can also use a number line to help us compare two numbers.

11 is greater than 6.   11 is less than 17.

0 1 2 3 4 5 ⑥ 7 8 9 10 ⑪ 12 13 14 15 16 ⑰ 18 19 20

Say What other statements can you make about the circled numbers on the number line?

Look at these number cards.

10 6 18 3 12 6

10 is less than 18.

6 is less than 10.   18 is greater than 12.   12 is more than 3.

Say What other statements can you make about the number cards?

Say What numbers could go in the boxes?

☐ is greater than 9.   ☐ is less than 14.

15 is more than ☐.   5 is less than ☐.

Pages 14–15, 24–25

Order objects and numbers to 20

Pages 6–13

We can use what we know about comparing two groups of objects or numbers to order groups of objects or a set of numbers. We can order the numbers from smallest to greatest or from greatest to smallest.

Count the crayons in each pot.

The orange pot has the **fewest** crayons.

The blue pot has the **most** crayons.

We can also say:

The blue pot has the **greatest** or **largest** amount of crayons.

The orange pot has the **smallest** or **least** amount of crayons.

smallest to greatest

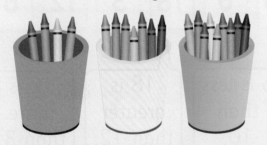

greatest to smallest

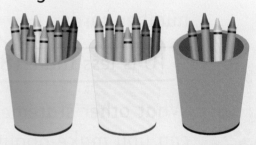

Say

Order the fruit from smallest to greatest.
What about from greatest to smallest?

We can order a set of numbers.

Which is the smallest number?

18 **4** **10**

Which is the greatest number?

We can use a number line to help order numbers.

4 is the smallest number.

18 is the greatest number.

0 1 2 3 ④ 5 6 7 8 9 ⑩ 11 12 13 14 15 16 17 ⑱ 19 20

We can also say: 18 is the largest number.

Where do these numbers sit on this number line?

12 **16** **3**

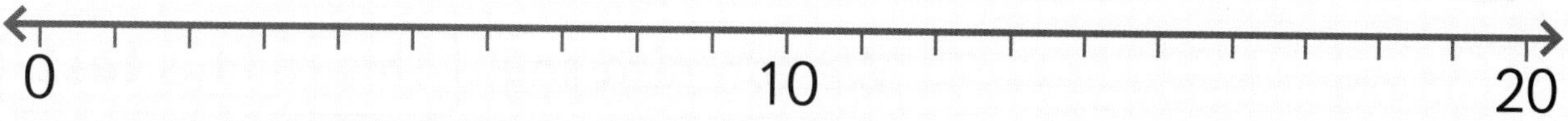

0   10   20

Say Order the numbers in each set. Start with the smallest number.

17 **9** **5** **13**

nineteen   two   six   fifteen

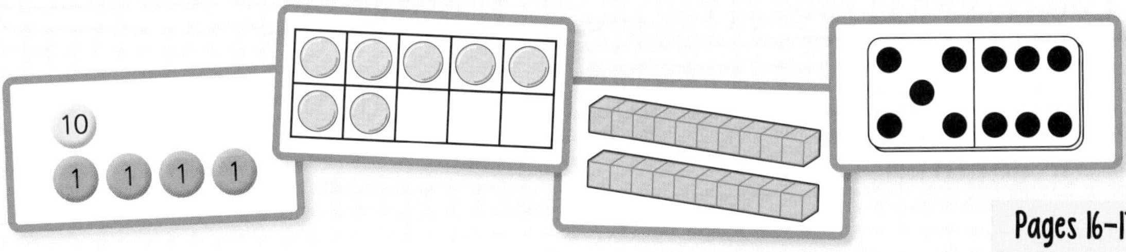

Pages 16-17, 26-27

Ordinal numbers

Pages 6–7, 14–15

Ordinal numbers are used to describe the place, position or order of someone or something.

Look at this row of children.

This child is **1st** in line.

2nd **3rd** **4th** **5th** **6th** **7th** **8th** **9th** **10th**

We can also say: This child is **last**.

We call these **ordinal numbers**.

1st	2nd	3rd	4th	5th	6th	7th	8th	9th	10th

Look at this line of children.

Ron is 5th in line.

The 9th child is Kim.

Sky	Leo	Sam	Mya	Ron	Joy	Kai	Tom	Kim	Lily

 Say What statements can you make about the line of children?

We can use ordinal numbers to describe **position**.

Look at this line of runners in a race.

first 1st
second 2nd
third 3rd
fourth 4th
fifth 5th
sixth 6th
seventh 7th
eighth 8th
ninth 9th
tenth 10th

The man in the blue top is 2nd.

The woman in the red top is 7th.

We can also say:

This runner is last.

 Say What statements can you make about the runners in the race?

 **Say** What statements can you make about the runners in this race?

Read, write and count numbers to 100

Pages 6–7

Once you can read, write and count numbers to 20, it's easy to extend this to numbers up to 100.

| 0 | 1 | 2 | 3 | 4 | 5 | 6 | 7 | 8 | 9 | 10 | 11 | 12 | 13 | 14 | 15 | 16 | 17 | 18 | 19 | 20 |

Say Point to a number in the **orange** column. Then to a number in the **green** column. Say your number.

20 twenty

30 thirty

40 forty

50 fifty

60 sixty

70 seventy

80 eighty

90 ninety

100 one hundred

45

1 one

2 two

3 three

4 four

5 five

6 six

7 seven

8 eight

9 nine

Look at the number 60.

60 means 6 **tens** or 6 **groups of** ten. → **60**

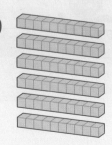

What do the numbers 30, 50, 80 and 100 mean?

We can use a 1–100 number square or number grid to help us **count on** and **count back**, **compare** and **order** numbers, and also see **patterns** in numbers.

What patterns can you see in this number square?

1	2	3	4	5	6	7	8	9	10
11	12	13	14	15	16	17	18	19	20
21	22	23	24	25	26	27	28	29	30
31	32	33	34	35	36	37	38	39	40
41	42	43	44	45	46	47	48	49	50
51	52	53	54	55	56	57	58	59	60
61	62	63	64	65	66	67	68	69	70
71	72	73	74	75	76	77	78	79	80
81	82	83	84	85	86	87	88	89	90
91	92	93	94	95	96	97	98	99	100

(Say) Choose two numbers on the 100 square.

Count **forwards** from the **smallest** number to the **largest** number.

Then count **backwards** from the largest number to the smallest number.

Pages 20–31

Represent numbers to 100

Pages 8–9, 18–19

We can show how many groups of tens and ones there are in a number to 100. Being able to split numbers into smaller parts makes them easier to work with.

We can use a part-whole model to split, or **partition**, numbers to 100 into two **parts**.

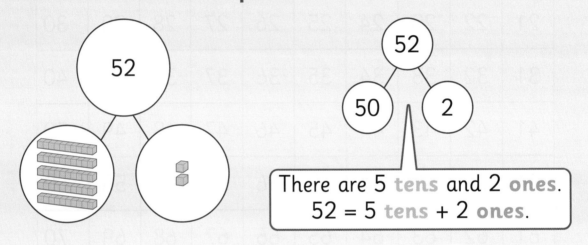

There are 5 **tens** and 2 **ones**.
52 = 5 **tens** + 2 **ones**.

Look at this place value chart.

To find the **value** of each **digit** we look at its position in the place value chart.

The digit 5 is in the **tens** position.

10s	1s
5	2

The digit 2 is in the **ones** position.

The **value** of the 5 is 5 **tens** or 50.

The value of the 2 is 2 **ones** or 2.

To find the whole number, we **add** the values together.

50 + 2 = 52

We can show 52 partitioned into **tens** and **ones** in lots of different ways.

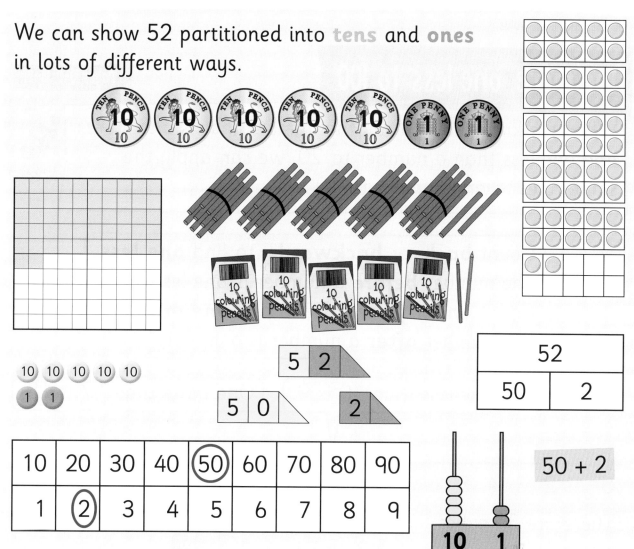

52	
50	2

5 | 2

5 | 0   2

$50 + 2$

10	20	30	40	50	60	70	80	90
1	2	3	4	5	6	7	8	9

11 to 100

Choose a number from 11 to 100.

How many different ways can you represent your number?

Build What objects could you use?

Draw What pictures or models might you draw?

Say Which part shows the **ones**?

Which part shows the **tens**?

How many **tens** and **ones** are there?

Pages 22–27

21

One more, one less to 100

Pages 10–11, 18–21

When we know how to say the number that is one more and one less than a number to 20, we can apply the same rules to any number to 100.

Remember
Count **back**, or **backwards**, to find **one less**.
The number **before** a number is one less.
Count **on**, or **forwards**, to find **one more**.
The number **after** a number is one more.

One less than 10 is 9.

One more than 17 is 18.

0 1 2 3 4 5 6 7 8 9 10 11 12 13 14 15 16 17 18 19 20

There are 37 cubes.

One less than 37 is 36.

One more than 37 is 38.

One less than 37 is 36.

| 31 | 32 | 33 | 34 | 35 | 36 | (37) | 38 | 39 | 40 |

One more than 37 is 38.

22

We can use a 1–100 number square to help us find the number that is one more or one less than a number.

1	2	3	4	5	6	7	8	9	10
11	12	13	14	15	16	17	18	19	20
21	22	23	24	25	26	27	28	29	30
31	32	33	34	35	36	(37)	38	39	40
41	42	43	44	45	46	47	48	49	50
51	52	53	54	55	56	57	58	59	60
61	62	63	64	65	66	67	68	69	70
71	72	73	74	75	76	77	78	79	80
81	82	83	84	85	86	87	88	89	90
91	92	93	94	95	96	97	98	99	100

One less than 37 is 36.

One more than 37 is 38.

 Say

1 to 99

Choose a number from 1 to 99. Then complete the sentences.

One more than ☐ is ☐. One less than ☐ is ☐.

☐ is one more than ☐. ☐ is one less than ☐.

Which **place value** column changes when you find one more or one less than a number?

10s	1s
3	7

10s	1s
4	9
2	9
7	9

What about when you find one more than 49, 29 or 79?

10s	1s
3	0
5	0
8	0

What about when you find one less than 30, 50 or 80?

Pages 24–25

Compare objects and numbers to 100

Pages 12–13, 18–23

To compare two groups of objects, we use words such as more, fewer or the same. To compare two numbers, we use words like greater than, less than or equal to.

Say Use the words **more** and **fewer** to **compare** these baskets of fruit.

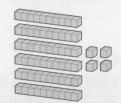

We can use objects and models to compare numbers.

| 10 | 10 | 10 | 10 | 10 | 10 | 10 |
| 1 | 1 |

is **greater than**

10s	1s
7	2

is **less than**

We can use a number line to help compare two numbers.

72 is greater than 64.   72 is less than 75.

60 61 62 63 (64) 65 66 67 68 69 70 71 (72) 73 74 (75) 76 77 78 79 80

We can also use signs, or symbols, to compare two numbers.

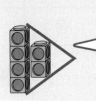

4 is greater than 2 or
4 is **more than** 2 or
4 is **larger than** 2.
4 > 2

2 is less than 4.
2 < 4

4 is **equal to** 4.
4 = 4

Look at the numbers circled on the number line on page 24.
We can say and write:

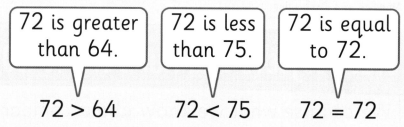

72 is greater than 64.

72 is less than 75.

72 is equal to 72.

72 > 64   72 < 75   72 = 72

It is important to remember what each of these symbols mean.

We can also say:

greater than

less than

equal to

more than or larger than

>

<

=

You might also say:

bigger than

the same as

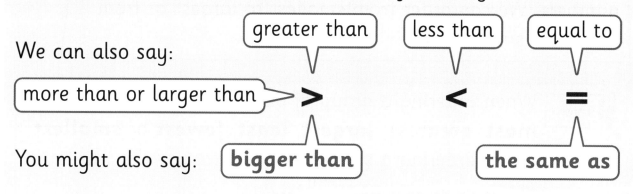

We can use a 1–100 number square to compare numbers to 100.

1	2	3	4	5	6	7	8	9	10
11	12	13	14	15	16	17	18	19	20
21	22	23	24	25	26	27	28	29	30
31	32	33	34	35	36	37	38	39	40
41	42	43	44	45	46	47	48	49	50
51	52	53	54	55	56	57	58	59	60
61	62	63	(64)	65	66	67	68	69	70
71	(72)	73	74	(75)	76	77	78	79	80
81	82	83	84	85	86	87	88	89	90
91	92	93	94	95	96	97	98	99	100

72 is greater than 64.

72 > 64

72 is less than 75.

72 < 75

Choose different pairs of numbers on the number square. What statements can you say and write, comparing each pair of numbers?

What numbers could go in the boxes?

☐ < 45   30 > ☐

☐ > 81   68 < ☐

Pages 26–27

Order objects and numbers to 100

Pages 14–15, 18–25

We can use what we know about comparing objects and numbers to 100 to order groups of objects or a set of numbers. We can order from smallest to largest or from largest to smallest.

Remember

When ordering a group of objects, we use the words: **most**, **greatest**, **largest**, **least**, **fewest** or **smallest**.

When ordering a set of numbers, we use the words: greatest, largest or smallest.

When ordering objects or numbers we might also say: **biggest**

Look at each group of Base 10.

We can **order** them from smallest to largest, or from largest to smallest.

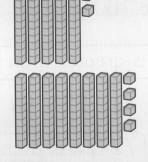

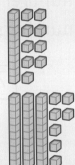

smallest to largest	largest to smallest
19 37 52 84	84 52 37 19

The four numbers above each have a different tens **digit**.

So, to order the numbers, we can just look at the tens digits.

Say Order each set of numbers from smallest to largest.

85	21	99	40		33	83	55	45

Look at this set of numbers.

There are two numbers with the same **tens** digit.

| 46 | 60 | 71 | 43 |

So, to order this set of numbers, we need to look at their **ones** digit.

The order of the four numbers from smallest to largest is:

| 43 | 46 | 60 | 71 |

Say Order each set of numbers. Start with the largest number.

| 28 | 55 | 80 | 52 |

| 36 | 73 | 63 | 37 |

We can use a 1–100 number square to order a set of numbers to 100.

The order of the numbers from largest to smallest is:

| 78 | 72 | 45 | 22 |

1	2	3	4	5	6	7	8	9	10
11	12	13	14	15	16	17	18	19	20
21	(22)	23	24	25	26	27	28	29	30
31	32	33	34	35	36	37	38	39	40
41	42	43	44	(45)	46	47	48	49	50
51	52	53	54	55	56	57	58	59	60
61	62	63	64	65	66	67	68	69	70
71	(72)	73	74	75	76	77	(78)	79	80
81	82	83	84	85	86	87	88	89	90
91	92	93	94	95	96	97	98	99	100

Look at these number tracks. What numbers could go in the empty boxes so that each number track is in order?

Write

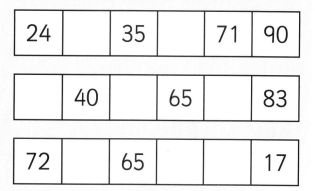

| 24 | | 35 | | 71 | 90 |

| | 40 | | 65 | | 83 |

| 72 | | 65 | | | 17 |

27

Count in 2s

Pages 18-19

Being able to count on and back in steps of 2 involves recognising and continuing number patterns, including the patterns of odd and even numbers.

What do you notice about the red numbers on the number line?

 Say Look at the red numbers:

- **Count on** along the number line from 0 to 20.
- Can you **count back** from 20 to 0?
- Starting from a red number other than 0, count on in 2s to 20.
- Starting from a red number other than 20, count back in 2s to 0.

We can use a number grid to **count in 2s** to 20.

1	2	3	4	5	6	7	8	9	10
11	12	13	14	15	16	17	18	19	20

We can also use this number line to count on and back in 2s.

0   2   4   6   8   10   12   14   16   18   20

We can count in 2s to find out how many socks there are.

1 group of 2 is **2**.   3 groups of 2 are **6**.

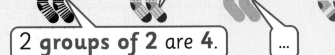

2 **groups** of **2** are **4**.   ...

Look at the cubes under the number line at the top of page 28.
Each set of cubes is made up of groups of 2 cubes.

> Numbers that can be made out of groups of 2 are called **even numbers**.

2 4 6 8 10 12 14 16 18 20

Look at the even numbers on the number lines and number grid on page 28.

What do you notice about the ones **digit** in each of the even numbers?

Look at the cubes under this number line.

What is different about these sets of cubes?

> Numbers that cannot be made out of groups of 2 are called **odd numbers**.

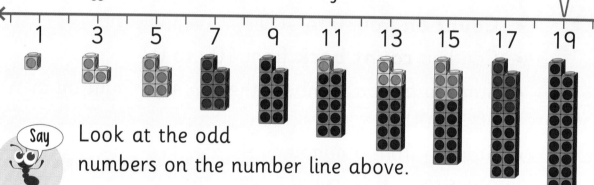

1   3   5   7   9   11   13   15   17   19

(Say) Look at the odd numbers on the number line above.

- Count on from 1 to 19.
- Can you count back from 19 to 1?
- Starting from a number other than 1, count on in 2s to 19.
- Starting from a number other than 19, count back in 2s to 1.

Can you use this 1–100 number square to count on and back in 2s?

What do you notice about the ones digit in each of the odd numbers?

1	2	3	4	5	6	7	8	9	10
11	12	13	14	15	16	17	18	19	20
21	22	23	24	25	26	27	28	29	30
31	32	33	34	35	36	37	38	39	40
41	42	43	44	45	46	47	48	49	50
51	52	53	54	55	56	57	58	59	60
61	62	63	64	65	66	67	68	69	70
71	72	73	74	75	76	77	78	79	80
81	82	83	84	85	86	87	88	89	90
91	92	93	94	95	96	97	98	99	100

Pages 30–31, 48–51

Count in 10s and 5s

Pages 18–19, 28–29

Just like counting in steps of 2, counting in steps of 10 and 5 involves recognising and continuing number patterns. Counting in steps – step counting – is important when multiplying or dividing.

Counting in steps of 10

What do you notice about the numbers on this number line?

```
←————————————————————————————————————————————→
   0   10   20   30   40   50   60   70   80   90   100
```

Say Look at the numbers on the number line.

- **Count on** from 0 to 100.
- Can you **count back** from 100 to 0?
- Starting from a number other than 0, count on in 10s to 100.
- Starting from a number other than 100, count back in 10s to 0.

1	2	3	4	5	6	7	8	9	10
11	12	13	14	15	16	17	18	19	20
21	22	23	24	25	26	27	28	29	30
31	32	33	34	35	36	37	38	39	40
41	42	43	44	45	46	47	48	49	50
51	52	53	54	55	56	57	58	59	60
61	62	63	64	65	66	67	68	69	70
71	72	73	74	75	76	77	78	79	80
81	82	83	84	85	86	87	88	89	90
91	92	93	94	95	96	97	98	99	100

We can use a 1–100 number square to **count in 10s** to 100.

We can count in tens to find out how many pencils there are.

We can say:

1 group of 10 is **10**.   3 groups of 10 are **30**.

2 **groups of 10** are **20**.   …

Counting in steps of 5

What do you notice about the numbers on this number line?

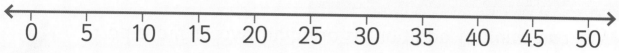

0   5   10   15   20   25   30   35   40   45   50

Say Look at the numbers on the number line.

- Count on from 0 to 50.
- Can you count back from 50 to 0?
- Starting from a number other than 0, count on in 5s to 50.
- Starting from a number other than 50, count back in 5s to 0.

We can use a number grid to **count in 5s** to 50.

We can count in fives to find out how many fingers there are.

We can say:

1	2	3	4	5	6	7	8	9	10
11	12	13	14	15	16	17	18	19	20
21	22	23	24	25	26	27	28	29	30
31	32	33	34	35	36	37	38	39	40
41	42	43	44	45	46	47	48	49	50

1 group of 5 is **5**.

3 groups of 5 are **15**.

2 groups of 5 are **10**.

...

Can you use this 1–100 number square to count on and back in 5s?

1	2	3	4	5	6	7	8	9	10
11	12	13	14	15	16	17	18	19	20
21	22	23	24	25	26	27	28	29	30
31	32	33	34	35	36	37	38	39	40
41	42	43	44	45	46	47	48	49	50
51	52	53	54	55	56	57	58	59	60
61	62	63	64	65	66	67	68	69	70
71	72	73	74	75	76	77	78	79	80
81	82	83	84	85	86	87	88	89	90
91	92	93	94	95	96	97	98	99	100

Pages 48–51

Addition as combining all

Pages 6-9

We can think of addition as bringing two or more parts together to make a whole, and counting them all.

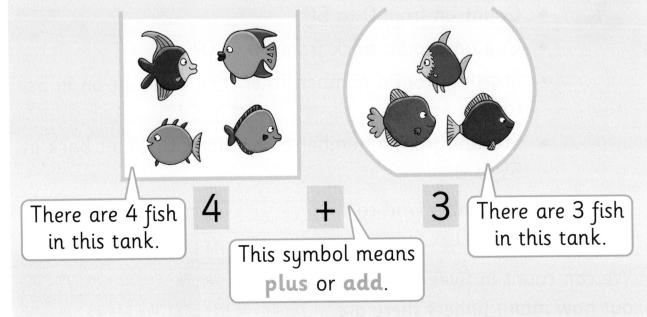

There are 4 fish in this tank.

4

+

This symbol means **plus** or **add**.

3

There are 3 fish in this tank.

If we count all the fish in both tanks, we know that there are 7 fish **altogether**.

We can say:

4 plus 3 **is equal to** 7.

or

4 add 3 **equals** 7.

We can also say:

The **total** of 4 and 3 is 7.

or

The **sum** of 4 and 3 is 7.

We can use different models to show this:

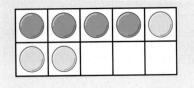

7	
4	3

4 is a part.

3 is a part.

7

4

3

7 is the whole.

We can write this as: **4 + 3 = 7**

This is called a **number sentence** or a **calculation**.

This symbol means **is the same as** or is equal to.

What does this picture show?

 **Say** How might you say this using some of these words:

| plus | add | sum | total |

| altogether | is the same as | equals |

 Build What objects could you use to show the same **addition**?

 Draw How might you draw this in a model?

 Write How would you write this as a number sentence?

 Addition is special. It doesn't matter which way we add the numbers, the total is always the same.

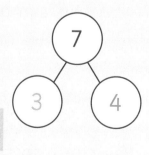

3 + 4 = 7 and **4 + 3 = 7**

We can also change the position of the equals symbol.

So, **7 = 3 + 4** and **7 = 4 + 3**

Pages 34–35, 42–43, 46–49

Addition as counting on

Pages 6–9, 32–33

Addition as counting on is when one group of objects is made greater by adding more.

Kim had 4 fish.
She bought 2 **more** fish.
How many fish does Kim have now?

First there were 4 fish.

Then 2 more fish were added.

Now there are 6 fish.

$$4 \quad + \quad 2 \quad = \quad 6$$

This symbol means **plus** or **add**.

This symbol means **is the same as** or **is equal to**.

We can say: 4 plus 2 is equal to 6. or 4 add 2 **equals** 6.

We can also say: 4 and 2 more is 6.

We can write this as an **addition number sentence**: $4 + 2 = 6$

When **counting on**, we can use a
number track or number line to help us.

$$4 + 2 = 6$$

Start at 4. Count on 2.

Equals 6.

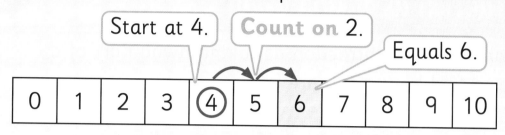

| 0 | 1 | 2 | 3 | ④ | 5 | 6 | 7 | 8 | 9 | 10 |

What does this picture show?

 **Say** How might you say
this using some of
these words?

plus   add   first, then, now

more   is the same as   equals

 Build What objects
could you use
to show the
same addition?

 Draw How might you show this
on a number line?

 Write How would you write this
as a number sentence?

 Look at the bottom of page 33. We know we can do an
addition in any order. Why might it be easier to start
with the **larger** number?

$$2 + 4 = 6$$

$$4 + 2 = 6$$

| 0 | 1 | 2 | 3 | ④ | 5 | 6 | 7 | 8 | 9 | 10 |

Pages 42–43, 46–53

Subtraction as taking away

Pages 6–9

We can think of subtraction as taking away part of a group to find how many are left.

There were 8 cakes on the cake stand.

Then 2 cakes were taken away.

Now there are 6 cakes **left** on the cake stand.

8 – 2 = 6

This symbol means **take away** or **subtract**.

This symbol means **is the same as** or **is equal to**.

We can write this as a **subtraction number sentence**:

$$8 - 2 = 6$$

We can say: 8 take away 2 is equal to 6. or 8 subtract 2 **equals** 6.

We can also say: 8 **minus** 2 is 6. or 8 minus 2 **leaves** 6.

We can show this as:

First there were 8 cakes.

8	
2	6

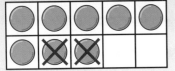

2 cakes were taken away.

Now there are 6 cakes left.

8

2   6

What do these pictures show?

 Say How might you say this using some of these words:

| take away | subtract | minus |

| is the same as | equals | leaves |

 Build What objects could you use to show the same subtraction?

 Draw How might you draw this in a model?

 Write How would you write this as a number sentence?

 **Write** Complete each of these number sentences in different ways.

6 − ☐ = ☐   ☐ − ☐ = 0

Pages 38–41, 44–47

Subtraction as counting back

Pages 6–9, 36–37

We can work out a subtraction by putting the start number in our head and counting backwards.

There were 9 people on the bus.

Then 4 people got off the bus.

Now there are 5 people left on the bus.

9   –   4   =   5

This symbol means **take away** or **subtract**.

This symbol means **is the same as** or **is equal to**.

We can write this as a **subtraction number sentence**:

$$9 - 4 = 5$$

We can say:

9 subtract 4 is equal to 5.

9 **minus** 4 is 5.

9 take away 4 **equals** 5.

For subtraction we can also say:

9 take away 4 **leaves** 5.

When **counting back**, we can use a number track or number line to help us.

Leaves 5.

Count back 4.

Start at 9.

0   1   2   3   4   ⑤   6   7   8   ⑨   10

What do these pictures show?

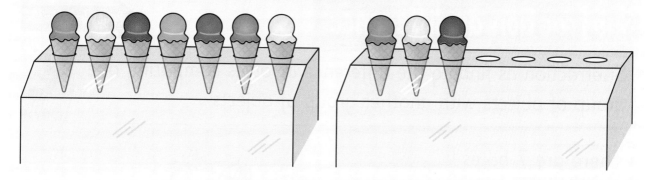

 Say How might you say this using some of these words?

| take away | subtract | minus |

| is the same as | equals | leaves |

 Build What objects could you use to show the same subtraction?

 Draw How might you show this on a number line?

 Write How would you write this as a number sentence?

 **Write** Write a number sentence for each of these number lines.

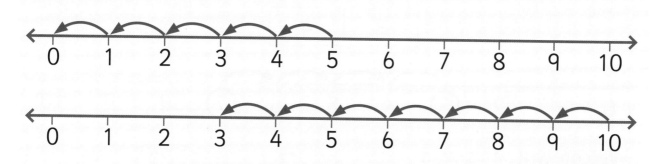

Pages 40–41, 44–47

Subtraction as difference

Pages 6–9, 36–39

Subtraction as finding the difference involves comparing one group of objects with another group of objects.

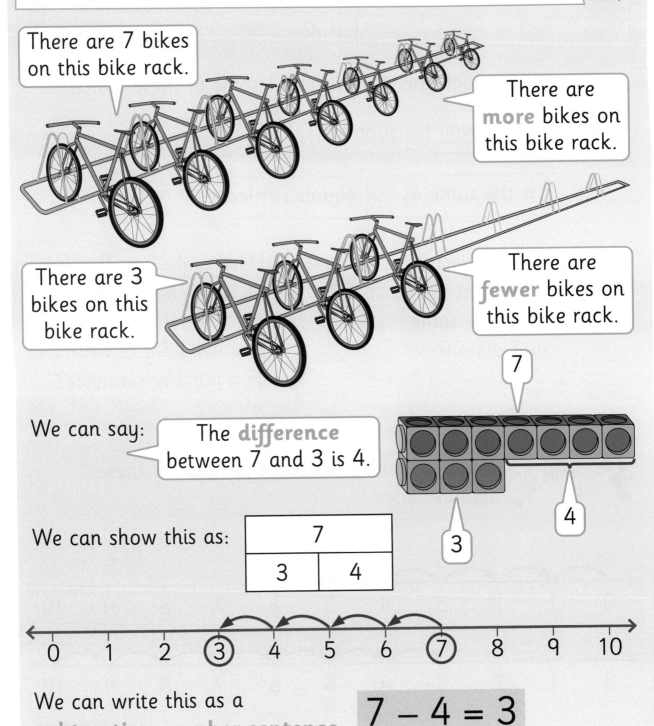

There are 7 bikes on this bike rack.

There are **more** bikes on this bike rack.

There are 3 bikes on this bike rack.

There are **fewer** bikes on this bike rack.

We can say: The **difference** between 7 and 3 is 4.

7

3

4

We can show this as:

7	
3	4

We can write this as a **subtraction number sentence**: $7 - 4 = 3$

40

When finding the difference, we can use a number track or number line to help us.

We can either **count back** or **count on** to find the difference.

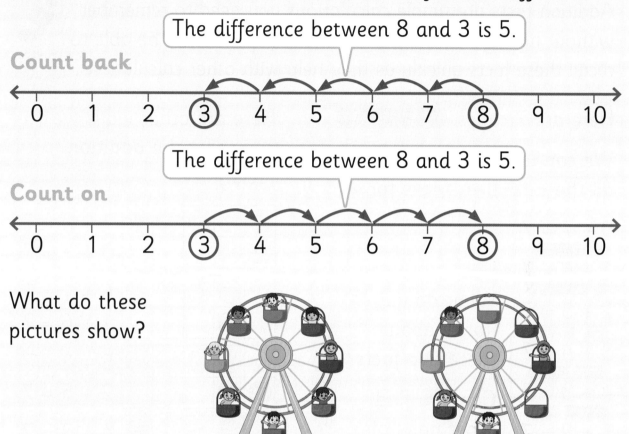

Count back

The difference between 8 and 3 is 5.

Count on

The difference between 8 and 3 is 5.

What do these pictures show?

Say How might you say this using some of these words?

| difference | more | fewer |

| is the same as | equals | leaves |

Build What objects could you use to show the same subtraction?

Draw How might you show this? What about on a number line?

Write How would you write this as a number sentence?

Pages 44–47

Addition facts to 10 and 20

Pages 6–11, 32–35

Addition facts are simple calculations you need to remember without having to work them out. It's important to be able to recall these facts quickly as they help with other calculations.

Here are 7 cubes.

We can use the cubes to find all the **addition facts** for 7.

0 + 7 = 7

1 + 6 = 7

2 + 5 = 7

3 + 4 = 7

4 + 3 = 7

5 + 2 = 7

6 + 1 = 7

7 + 0 = 7

What do you notice about these two facts?

Can you find other pairs of facts like this?

Here are other ways we can show the addition facts for 7.

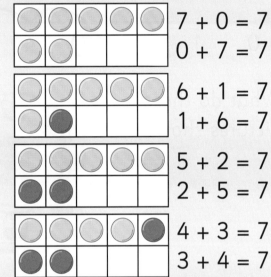

7 + 0 = 7
0 + 7 = 7

6 + 1 = 7
1 + 6 = 7

5 + 2 = 7
2 + 5 = 7

4 + 3 = 7
3 + 4 = 7

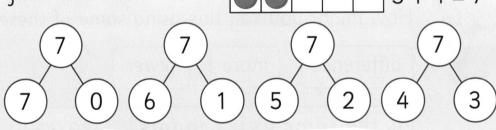

Here are 8 beads.

Build

Use beads or other objects to show all the addition facts for 8.

Draw

How might you draw these in a model?

Write

How would you write these as number sentences?

Remember Addition can be done in any order. This can help when we **add** numbers.

Recalling the addition facts to 10 can help us work out the addition facts to 20.

$9 + 7 = 16$

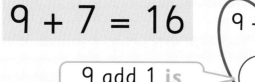

9 add 1 **is equal to** 10.

10 **plus** 6 **equals** 16.

We can use a number line or ten frames.

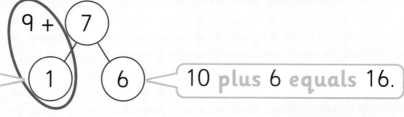

$13 + 4 = 17$

If ➤ $3 + 4 = 7$ then ➤ $13 + 4 = 17$

 If ➤ then ➤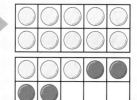

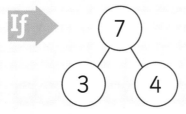

If ➤ then ➤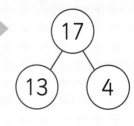

 Build Use objects to show each of these addition facts to 20.

 Draw How might you draw these in a model?

$6 + 8 = \boxed{}$ $3 + 15 = \boxed{}$

Pages 46–47, 52–53

Subtraction facts to 10 and 20

Pages 6–11, 36–41

It's important to be able to recall the subtraction facts to 10, and then to 20. Once we know these facts, we can then use them to answer other calculations.

We can use cubes to show the **subtraction facts** for 7, like on page 42, where we used cubes to find the addition facts for 7.

$7 - 0 = 7$

$7 - 1 = 6$

$7 - 2 = 5$

$7 - 3 = 4$

$7 - 4 = 3$

$7 - 5 = 2$

$7 - 6 = 1$

$7 - 7 = 0$

What do you notice about these two facts?

Can you find other pairs of facts like this?

Here are other ways we can show the subtraction facts for 7.

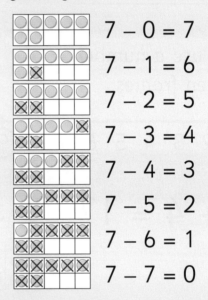

$7 - 0 = 7$

$7 - 1 = 6$

$7 - 2 = 5$

$7 - 3 = 4$

$7 - 4 = 3$

$7 - 5 = 2$

$7 - 6 = 1$

$7 - 7 = 0$

(7) (7) (0) (6) (1) (5) (2) (4) (3)

Here are 8 beads.

 Build Use beads or other objects to show all the subtraction facts for 8.

 Draw How might you draw these in a model?

 Write How would you write these as number sentences?

Recalling the subtraction facts to 10 helps with knowing subtraction facts to 20.

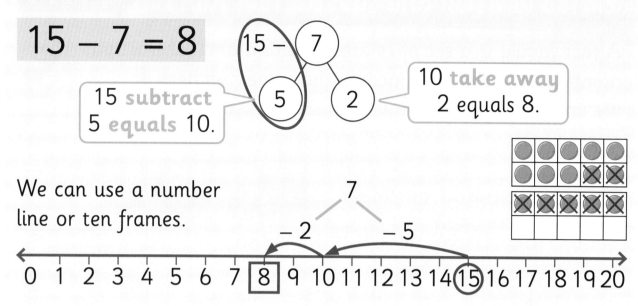

$$15 - 7 = 8$$

15 **subtract** 5 **equals** 10.

10 **take away** 2 equals 8.

We can use a number line or ten frames.

7

$- 2$ $- 5$

0 1 2 3 4 5 6 7 8 9 10 11 12 13 14 15 16 17 18 19 20

 Remember We can think of subtraction as finding the **difference**. This means **comparing** one group of objects with another group of objects.

$$14 - 5 = 9$$

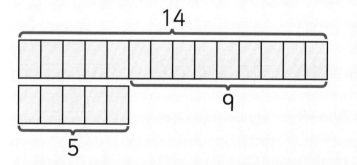

14

5 | 9

 Build Use objects to show each of these subtraction facts to 20.

 Draw How might you draw these in a model?

$$17 - 8 = \boxed{}$$ $$19 - 5 = \boxed{}$$

Pages 46–47

Related addition and subtraction facts

Pages 6–11, 32–45

A fact family is a set of related addition and subtraction number sentences that include the same numbers. If we know one fact, then we can use this to recall other related facts.

How many frogs **altogether**?

We can use different models to show this:

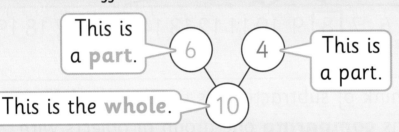

This is a **part**. — 6   4 — This is a part.

This is the **whole**. — 10

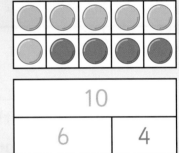

	10	
6		4

From the picture and models above, we can write these related **addition** and **subtraction** number sentences:

We can write the addition **number sentence**:

Addition can be done in any order. So, we can also write:

We can also write this as two subtraction number sentences:

$6 + 4 = 10$	$10 = 6 + 4$
$4 + 6 = 10$	$10 = 4 + 6$
$10 - 4 = 6$	$6 = 10 - 4$
$10 - 6 = 4$	$4 = 10 - 6$

Remember

We're all a **fact family**.

= means **is the same as** or **is equal to**. So, we can also write these four facts.

 Write   Write the fact family for this part-whole model.

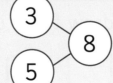

3
5
8

We can use fact families to help solve missing number problems.

What is the **value** of the **missing part** in each of these number sentences?

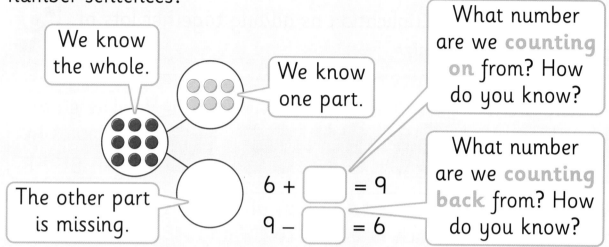

We know the whole.

We know one part.

The other part is missing.

What number are we **counting on** from? How do you know?

What number are we **counting back** from? How do you know?

$6 + \boxed{} = 9$

$9 - \boxed{} = 6$

How would you work out the value of the missing part in each of these number sentences?

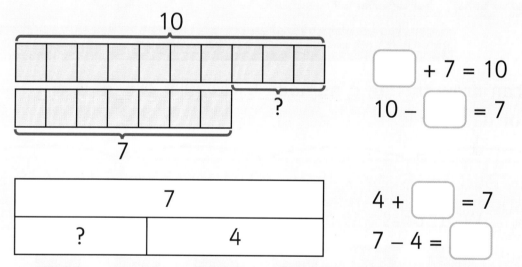

10

?

7

7

? | 4

$\boxed{} + 7 = 10$

$10 - \boxed{} = 7$

$4 + \boxed{} = 7$

$7 - 4 = \boxed{}$

Work out the value of the missing part in these number sentences.

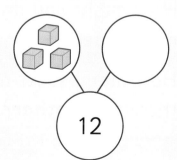

12

$3 + \boxed{} = 12$

$12 - 3 = \boxed{}$

$\boxed{} + 3 = 12$

$12 - \boxed{} = 3$

Multiplication as repeated addition

Pages 6–7, 28–35

We can think of multiplication as adding together lots of groups of the same size.

There are 4 **equal groups** of apples.

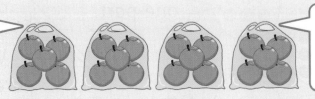

There are 5 apples **in each group**.

We can say: There are 4 groups of 5 apples which **is equal to** 20 apples.

We can show this in different ways:

We can draw this on a number line or as a model.

0 1 2 3 4 5 6 7 8 9 10 11 12 13 14 15 16 17 18 19 20

Say What does this picture show?

Build What objects could you use to show this?

Draw How might you draw this in a model?

How many socks are there **altogether**?

Remember Think about counting in steps of 2.

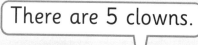 There are 5 clowns.

 Each clown has 2 balloons.

There are 2 **plus** 2 plus 2 plus 2 plus 2 balloons. There are 5 groups of 2 balloons which is equal to 10 balloons.

We can show this in different ways:

2	2	2	2	2

So, we can write this as an **addition number sentence**.

$$2 + 2 + 2 + 2 + 2 = 10$$

 Say What does this picture show?

 Build What objects could you use to show this?

 Draw How might you draw this in a model?

 Remember Think about counting in steps of 10.

 Write How would you write this as an addition number sentence?

Pages 50–53

Multiplication as an array

Pages 6–7, 28–31, 34–35, 48–49

We can arrange groups of the same size into rows and columns. We call this an array.

There are 5 chocolates in each **row**.

There are 4 rows of chocolates.

We can write this as an **addition number sentence**.

$$5 + 5 + 5 + 5 = 20$$

We can see this box of chocolates in a different way.

There are 4 chocolates in each **column**.

There are 5 columns of chocolates.

We can write this as an addition number sentence.

$$4 + 4 + 4 + 4 + 4 = 20$$

We can use objects to show how many chocolates there are altogether.

We can also draw a model called an **array**.

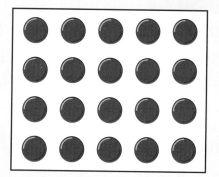

Look at the box of doughnuts.

How many **equal groups** of doughnuts are there?

How many doughnuts are **in each group**?

How many doughnuts are in each row? How many rows are there?

How many doughnuts are in each column? How many columns are there?

Build How could you show this using objects such as interlocking cubes or counters?

Draw How would you draw this as an array?

Write How could you write this as an addition number sentence?

51

Doubles

Pages 6–7, 34–35, 42–43, 48–49

Double means two equal groups of objects or two of the same number. If you double something, you make it twice as big or twice as much.

This ladybird has 3 spots.

This ladybird has **double** that number of spots. It has 6 spots.

We say: Double 3 is 6.

We can use objects to show that double 3 is 6.

We can show this in a ten frame:

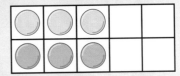

We can write this as an **addition number sentence**: 3 + 3 = 6

Double the number of pieces of fruit on each plate.

Look at one of the plates of fruit on page 52.

 Use objects to show its double.

 Show this in a ten frame.

 Write this as an addition number sentence.

Look at these doubles.

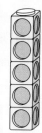 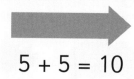 Double 5 is 10.

$5 + 5 = 10$

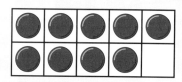 Double 9 is 18.

$9 + 9 = 18$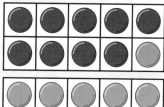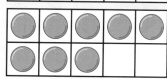

Double 7 is 14.

 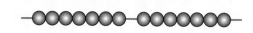

$7 + 7 = 14$

Look at these doubles.

Double 6 is ⬚.   Double 8 is ⬚.   Double 10 is ⬚.

 Use objects to show each double.

 Show each double in a model.

 Write each double as an addition number sentence.

Pages 58–59

Division as sharing

Pages 6–7

Division as sharing is when a group of objects is shared equally between a known number of groups, and we need to find out how many objects belong in each group.

There were 15 marbles in the box.
They were **shared equally between** 5 children.
Each child got 3 marbles.

15 marbles

We can say: **15 divided between 5 is equal to 3 each.**

We can also say: 15 shared equally between 5 is 3.

We can use different models to show this:

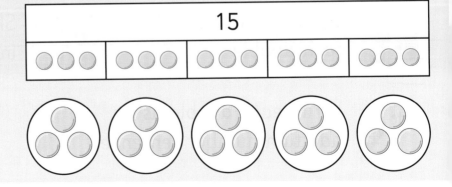

54

There are 20 cherries.
They are shared equally
between 2 children.
How many cherries does
each child get?

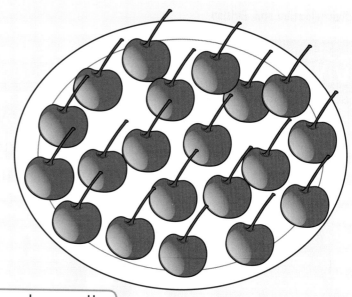

We can say:

20 divided between 2
is equal to 10 each.

We can also say: 20 shared equally
between 2 is 10.

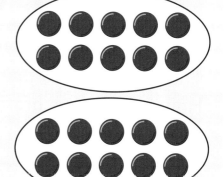

We can use different models to show this:

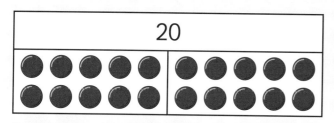

 How would you share the 20 cherries equally between
5 children?

 How would
you say this?

 How could you draw
this in a model?

 How would you share the 20 cherries equally between
10 children?

 How would
you say this?

 How could you draw
this in a model?

Pages 58–61

Division as grouping

Pages 6–7

Division as grouping is when we know the total number of objects, and how many objects belong in each group, and we need to find out how many equal groups there are.

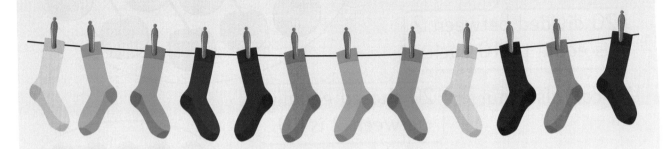

There are 12 socks on a line.
They are put into pairs.
How many pairs are there?

Pairs are **equal groups of** 2.

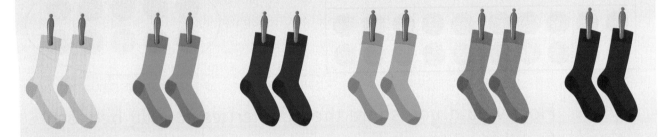

We can say:
12 has been **divided into groups of** 2.
There are 6 **groups**.

We can also say:
There are 6 equal groups of 2 in 12.

We can use different models to show this:

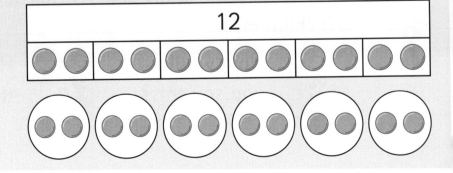

Miko's chickens lay 12 eggs.
Each box has space for 4 eggs.
How many boxes does he need?

We can say:

12 has been divided into groups of 4.
There are 3 groups.

We can also say: There are 3 equal groups of 4 in 12.

We can use different models to show this:

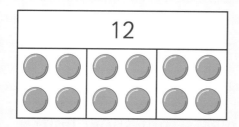

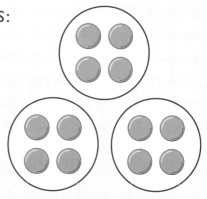

 How many equal groups of 6 would Miko get from the 12 eggs?

 Say How would you say this?

Draw How could you draw this in a model?

 How many equal groups of 3 would Miko get from the 12 eggs?

 Say How would you say this?

 Draw How could you draw this in a model?

Pages 58–61

Half

Pages 6–7, 52–57

A fraction is part of a whole. When we split a whole into 2 equal parts, we call each of the 2 parts a half.

The **whole** cake.

The whole cake has been cut into **2 equal parts**.

Each slice of the cake is **half** of the whole cake.

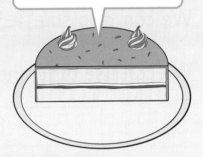

Look at each of these shapes and objects.

Can you spot the shapes and objects that show half?

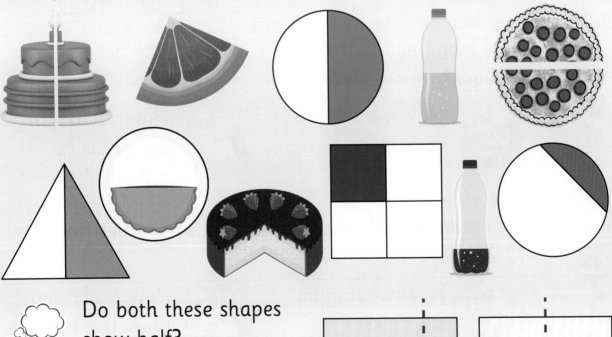

Do both these shapes show half?

Can you explain why?

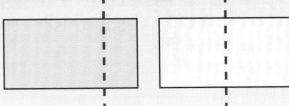

We can find half of a shape or an object. We can also find half of a group of objects.

There are 8 cubes in each whole tower.

The red part of this tower is NOT half.

The red part of this tower is NOT half.

The red part of this tower is half.

Half of 8 is 4.

These are the steps to find half of a group of objects:

1. Count the total number of objects – the whole.

2. Share the whole into 2 equal parts.

3. Count the number of objects in 1 part.

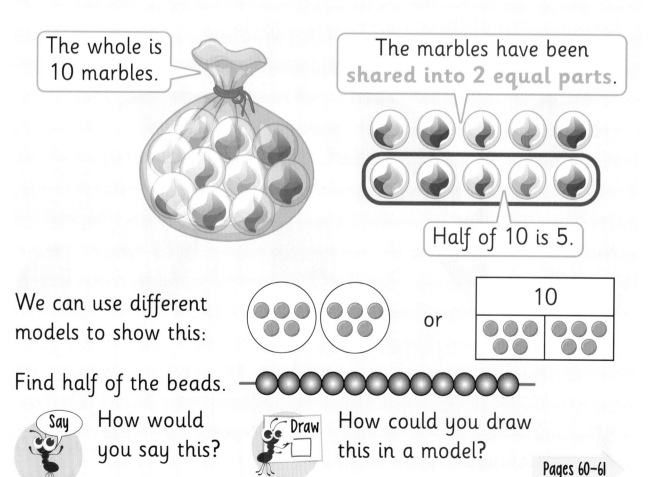

The whole is 10 marbles.

The marbles have been shared into 2 equal parts.

Half of 10 is 5.

We can use different models to show this:

or

10

Find half of the beads.

Say How would you say this?

Draw How could you draw this in a model?

Pages 60–61

Quarter

Pages 6–7, 54–59

A quarter is one of 4 equal parts. We can find a quarter of a shape, an object or a group of objects.

The **whole** cake.

The whole cake has been cut into **4 equal parts**.

Each slice of the cake is a **quarter** of the whole cake.

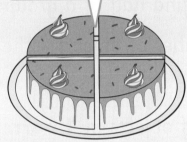
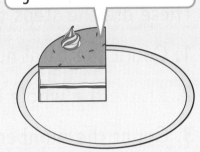

Look at each of these shapes and objects.

Can you spot the shapes and objects that show a quarter?

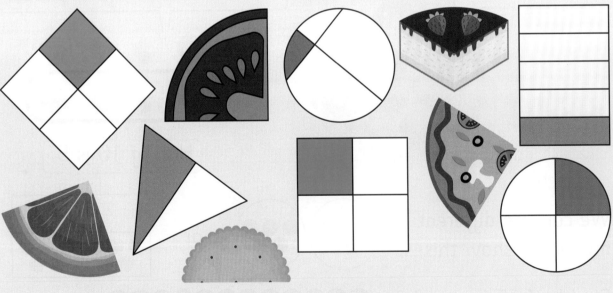

Do both these shapes show a quarter?

Can you explain why?

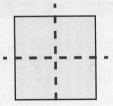
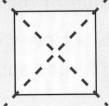

Let's look at finding a quarter of a group of objects.

There are 8 cubes in each whole block of cubes.

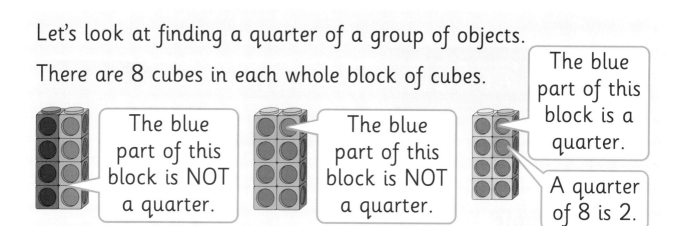

The blue part of this block is NOT a quarter.

The blue part of this block is NOT a quarter.

The blue part of this block is a quarter.

A quarter of 8 is 2.

These are the steps to find a quarter of a group of objects:

1. Count the total number of objects – the whole.

2. Share the whole into 4 equal parts.

3. Count the number of objects in 1 part.

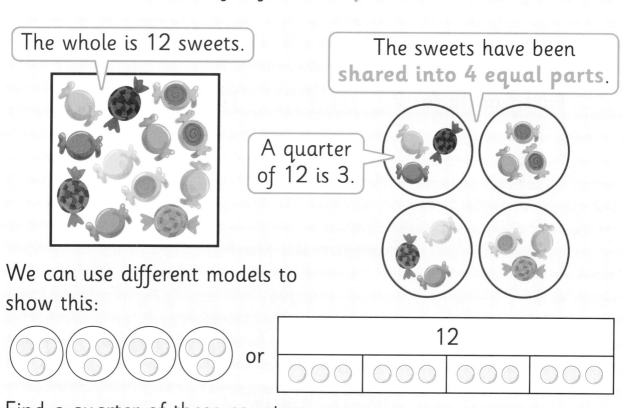

The whole is 12 sweets.

The sweets have been shared into 4 equal parts.

A quarter of 12 is 3.

We can use different models to show this:

or

12			

Find a quarter of these counters.

Say

How would you say this?

Draw

How could you draw this in a model?

Year I Number facts

Addition and subtraction facts to 10

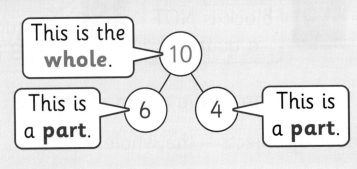

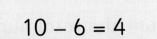

$6 + 4 = 10$

$4 + 6 = 10$

$10 - 4 = 6$

$10 - 6 = 4$

Fact family for 0

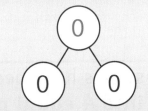

Fact family for 1

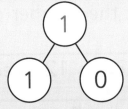

Fact family for 2

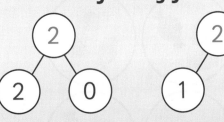

Fact family for 3

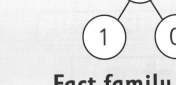

Fact family for 4

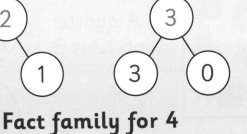

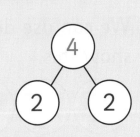

Fact family for 5

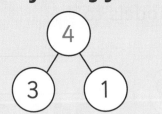

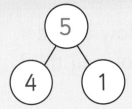

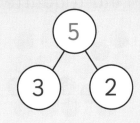

Fact family for 6

6 → 6, 0
6 → 5, 1
6 → 4, 2
6 → 3, 3

Fact family for 7

7 → 7, 0
7 → 6, 1
7 → 5, 2
7 → 4, 3

Fact family for 8

8 → 8, 0
8 → 7, 1
8 → 6, 2
8 → 5, 3
8 → 4, 4

Fact family for 9

9 → 9, 0
9 → 8, 1
9 → 7, 2
9 → 6, 3
9 → 5, 4

Fact family for 10

10 → 10, 0
10 → 9, 1
10 → 8, 2
10 → 7, 3
10 → 6, 4
10 → 5, 5

Multiplication and division facts

Counting in steps of 2

0 2 4 6 8 10 12 14 16 18 20

1	2	3	4	5	6	7	8	9	10
11	12	13	14	15	16	17	18	19	20

Counting in steps of 5

0 5 10 15 20 25 30 35 40 45 50

1	2	3	4	5	6	7	8	9	10
11	12	13	14	15	16	17	18	19	20
21	22	23	24	25	26	27	28	29	30
31	32	33	34	35	36	37	38	39	40
41	42	43	44	45	46	47	48	49	50

Counting in steps of 10

0 10 20 30 40 50 60 70 80 90 100

1	2	3	4	5	6	7	8	9	10
11	12	13	14	15	16	17	18	19	20
21	22	23	24	25	26	27	28	29	30
31	32	33	34	35	36	37	38	39	40
41	42	43	44	45	46	47	48	49	50
51	52	53	54	55	56	57	58	59	60
61	62	63	64	65	66	67	68	69	70
71	72	73	74	75	76	77	78	79	80
81	82	83	84	85	86	87	88	89	90
91	92	93	94	95	96	97	98	99	100